SOLVE IT WITH SCIENCE

VIOLENT CRIMES

JON SUTHERLAND
AND
DIANE CANWELL

W

FRANKLIN WATTS
LONDON • SYDNEY

First published in 2009 by Franklin Watts

Copyright © 2009 Arcturus Publishing Limited

Franklin Watts
338 Euston Road
London NW1 3BH

Franklin Watts Australia
Level 17/207 Kent Street, Sydney, NSW 2000

Produced by Arcturus Publishing Limited,
26/27 Bickels Yard, 151–153 Bermondsey Street,
London SE1 3HA

Series concept: Alex Woolf
Editor and picture researcher: Alex Woolf
Designer: Tall Tree

The illustrations on pages 32, 34 and 38 are by
Jason Line.

A CIP catalogue record for this book is available from
the British Library.

Dewey Decimal Classification Number: 364.15

ISBN 978 0 7496 8755 7

Printed in China

Franklin Watts is a division of Hachette Children's
Books, an Hachette UK company.
www.hachette.co.uk

Picture credits:
Arcturus Publishing: 32, 34, 38.
Corbis: 4 (Ron Chapple Stock), 6 (Ashley Cooper), 16
(Bettmann), 17 (Bettmann), cover *right* and 20
(Bettmann), 23 (Bettmann), 28 (Bettmann), 30
(Bettmann), 40 (Global TV/Handout/Reuters), 42
(Reuters).
Getty: 8 (Topical Press Agency/Stringer), 9 (Bentley
Archive/Popperfoto), 12 (Popperfoto), 13
(Popperfoto), 14 (Bentley Archive/Popperfoto), 15
(Popperfoto), 18 (Time & Life Pictures/Art Shay), 19
(Time & Life Pictures/Dick Swanson), 25 (Time & Life
Pictures/Evelyn Floret).
PA Photos: 22 (AP Photo), 24 (AP Photo/Bob Lucky Jr),
41 (AP Photo/CP).
Rex Features: 5.
Science Photo Library: 7 (Philippe Psaila), 10 (Ria
Novosti), 11 (Volker Steger), 21 (Andrew Syred), 27
(Mauro Fermariello), 29 (Mauro Fermariello), 31
(Mauro Fermariello), 33 (Mauro Fermariello), 35
(Martin Shields), 37 (Bruno Petriglia), 39 (Volker
Steger), 43 (Volker Steger).
Shutterstock: cover *knife* (Dmitrijs Mihejevs), cover *axe*
(Dmitry Rukhlenko), cover *gloves* (Cekuro).

Every attempt has been made to clear copyright.
Should there be any inadvertent omission, please
apply to the publisher for rectification.

CONTENTS

INTRODUCTION

When someone uses force on a victim, this is a violent crime. Murder, robbery, assault and kidnapping are all violent crimes. Such crimes often involve the use of a gun or a knife. The most serious type of violent crime is the killing of another human being.

FAMOUS VIOLENT CRIMES

History is littered with violent crimes. In 19th-century Scotland William Burke and William Hare murdered people so that they could sell the bodies to doctors for medical experiments.

In the United States in the 1920s gangsters were involved in many violent crimes. One of the most famous, and violent, gangsters was Al Capone. There were violent gangsters in

Murderers often make great efforts to remove the evidence of their crimes.

4

London, too. In the 1960s the Kray twins and the Richardson family were involved in hijacks, armed robbery and gang killings.

Not all violent crimes are carried out for money. The nurse Beverley Allitt became known as the Angel of Death. She killed four small children in the 1990s. Her motives for doing so have never been fully understood.

Some commit violent crimes for love. Ruth Ellis shot and killed her boyfriend after an argument. She was hanged in 1955, the last woman in England to face the death penalty.

FORENSICS AND VIOLENT CRIME

Many different forensic techniques are used to help solve violent crimes. Forensic scientists may be able to find evidence at the crime scene. They are specially trained to look for things that other people may not even notice.

SERIAL KILLERS

Among the most notorious violent crimes are those carried out by serial killers. Dennis Nilsen, for example, killed 15 people in five years. Peter Sutcliffe, who murdered 13 women over six years, became known as the Yorkshire Ripper.

Peter Sutcliffe killed 13 women and attacked several others in West Yorkshire, UK, between 1975 and 1981.

There may be fingerprints, footprints, tyre tracks, chips of paint, soil and fibres. There may also be biological evidence such as blood, hair or fingernails. Sometimes forensic scientists find evidence of the weapon that was used. This might be a bullet or knife marks. All these things are known as **trace evidence**, and they are highly important in solving violent crimes.

Samples of trace evidence are collected by brushing, vacuuming or swabbing the crime scene. Samples are collected in bags, carefully labelled and then taken back to the laboratory. Forensic scientists then analyse the samples to help them understand what happened and who may have committed the crime.

IDENTIFYING VICTIMS AND SUSPECTS

If the crime scene is old, then other forensic techniques can be used. **Forensic anthropology** involves the study of skeletons and other human remains to discover the identity of a victim.

Sometimes forensic dentistry is used to identify victims. Evidence from a victim's teeth can be compared with the dental records of missing people to try and find a match. **Forensic odontologists** can also help to identify a suspect

Forensic scientists search for evidence at a crime scene. They wear protective clothing, gloves and masks to ensure they don't contaminate the evidence.

A forensic entomologist uses a microscope to analyse a fly found on the body of a murder victim.

from teeth marks that may have been left in a victim or in discarded food found at the crime scene.

TIME, PLACE AND CAUSE OF DEATH

Forensic entomology is the study of insects found in or around a body to establish the time or place of death. **Pathologists** try to discover the cause of death by examining the bodies of victims.

DNA PROFILING

DNA is the chemical material that holds the instructions for making a particular person. DNA is like a fingerprint – everyone's DNA is slightly different. Every cell in your body, including blood, saliva, skin and hair, contains DNA. It can be gathered from eating utensils, clothing and other items found at crime scenes. DNA profiling was developed in the 1980s. Since then, it has provided vital evidence in many cases, linking suspects to crime scenes.

THE JIGSAW MURDERS

Buck Ruxton was born in Bombay, India, in 1899. In 1930 he moved to Lancaster in the UK, where he set himself up as a doctor. He married a woman called Isabella, a sociable and popular lady in the local community.

Dr Buck Ruxton was a respected doctor, and well liked by his patients.

THE JEALOUS DOCTOR

Ruxton was jealous of his wife's popularity and came to believe she was having an affair. On 15 September 1935 he strangled Isabella. Because her maid Mary Rogerson had witnessed his crime, he killed her too. He cut the bodies up, put them in his car, then drove through the night to Scotland, 160 kilometres to the north. Here he dumped the body parts in a stream.

THE OBSERVANT CYCLIST

Near Kendal, on his return journey from Scotland, Ruxton knocked over a cyclist called Bernard Beattie. Ruxton did not stop, but the cyclist took a note of the car's number plate. The registration matched Ruxton's. The doctor later denied he had driven to Scotland that night, but Beattie's statement provided strong evidence to the contrary.

Mary Rogerson's mother reported her missing to the police. They visited Ruxton to ask about her, but he said she had not been to work for two days. A few days later the police returned to Ruxton because Isabella's friends had reported her missing. He told the police that Isabella had gone away with her lover.

SURPRISE PACKAGE
Not long afterwards body remains were found in a ravine in Moffat, Scotland. The body parts were wrapped in a copy of a newspaper that was only sold in Lancashire – a

vital clue that the police were quick to follow up on. The body parts were sent to the University of Edinburgh for a **post-mortem** examination. It was established that the bodies belonged to two women, one a young lady and the other in her forties.

Police search for evidence at the ravine in Moffat, Scotland, where the two bodies were discovered.

The tips of the women's fingers had been removed to prevent fingerprint identification. However, police suspected that the dead bodies belonged to the missing women, Isabella Ruxton and Mary Rogerson. It was now up to forensic scientists to try to prove it.

NEW TECHNIQUES

A team of forensic scientists was assembled, led by the **pathologist** John Glaister and the **anatomist** James Couper Brash. They used several new techniques to match the remains to Isabella and Mary.

The scientists decided to reconstruct the bodies from scratch. They did this by matching each part to any known distinguishing features of the women. They **x-rayed** the skulls and then **superimposed** tracings from photographs of each woman on the x-rays. Eventually they managed to reconstruct two

skeletons from the various body parts. Because the jumbled body parts had to be reassembled, the case became known as the 'jigsaw murders'.

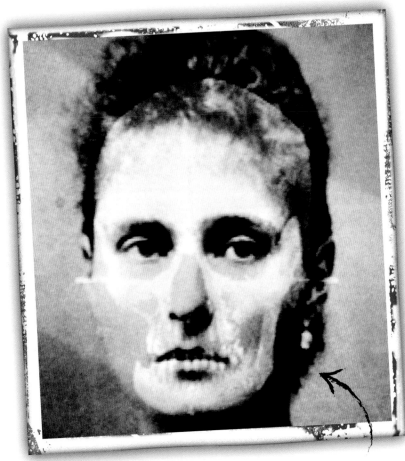

Forensic scientists used techniques similar to those employed in the Buck Ruxton case to match skull fragments to Tsarina Alexandra of Russia (1872–1918). A photo of the tsarina was superimposed on an x-ray of the skull fragments.

PHOTOGRAPHING THE SKULLS

It was Professor Brash who came up with the idea of x-raying the skulls. He had photographs of Isabella and Mary blown up to life size. This allowed him to trace the facial characteristics of each of the women onto transparent paper. By placing the transparent paper over the x-rays he could match the facial characteristics of Isabella and Mary to the x-rays of the skulls.

The scientists also used forensic entomology – the study of insects in criminal investigations – a science still in its infancy in 1935. Larvae found in the body parts were taken to the laboratory and the larvae's age was established. The age fitted perfectly with the date that the bodies had been dumped.

A blowfly larva feeds on liver tissue.
The length of the blowfly's life cycle from egg to fly varies according to temperature, so the size of the larva and temperature can be used to calculate time of death.

TRIAL

Ruxton was arrested on 13 October. During his trial, Glaister and Brash gave their evidence. It was the first time their pioneering forensic techniques had been used as evidence in a court of law. The forensic evidence proved to be crucial. Buck Ruxton was found guilty of murdering the two women. He was hanged in Manchester on 12 May 1936.

THE ACID BATH MURDERS

John George Haigh was born in Yorkshire in 1909. During his 20s and early 30s, he went to prison several times for fraud and theft. After his release from prison in 1944, he started to commit murders.

John George Haigh, the Acid Bath Murderer.

DISPOSING OF THE BODIES

On 9 September 1944 he hit his employer and friend William McSwan over the head and then slit his throat. Haigh put the body in a large metal drum and filled it with concentrated **sulphuric acid**. He wore a gas mask and rubber clothes to protect himself from the acid. By the following day, the body had turned to sludge, which Haigh poured down a drain.

Haigh told McSwan's parents that their son had gone to Scotland. When the parents became suspicious, he killed them too, on 2 July 1945, and dissolved their bodies in acid. He forged William McSwan's signature on legal documents so he could sell his and his parents' possessions and receive their pensions. Haigh moved into an expensive hotel, the Onslow Court in Kensington, London.

THE EFFECTS OF ACID

Haigh believed that dissolving his victims in acid would destroy any evidence of the bodies. But he was wrong. Certain parts of the human body, such as bone and fat, do not dissolve so quickly or easily. Also, artificial items belonging to his victims, such as false teeth, would later be discovered and used as evidence by forensic scientists.

bodies in acid. Haigh forged documents to get at the couple's money. Then, at the Onslow Court, he met a wealthy elderly woman, Mrs Olive Durand-Deacon. Very soon she was also dead.

MORE VICTIMS

An addicted gambler, Haigh soon began to run out of money. He looked around for someone else to kill and steal from. In 1947 he befriended Dr Archibald Henderson and his wife Rose. In February 1948 he shot them both. Again he dissolved both

Dr Archibald and Rose Henderson were both victims of Haigh.

ARRESTED

Haigh sold her jewellery and fur coat, worth a total of £110. Durand-Deacon's friend Constance Lane reported her disappearance to the police. The police interviewed people at the hotel. They soon discovered Haigh's criminal record and became suspicious. The police searched Haigh's storehouse in Crawley. Here they found a revolver and eight bullets. On 2 March 1949 Haigh was arrested.

Dr Keith Simpson, a government pathologist, searches for evidence in a pile of burnt rubbish at Haigh's Crawley storehouse.

Haigh confessed to the killings. He told the police he had dissolved the bodies in acid after drinking their blood. Several doctors and psychologists had interviewed him about his claims of needing to drink blood. They decided he had committed the murders for his own gains and had pretended to be insane when he was caught.

REMAINS DISCOVERED

Despite Haigh's efforts to dissolve the bodies, traces of human remains were found by forensic scientists. These included body fat and fragments of bone. Part of Olive Durand-Deacon's left foot was discovered and a cast was

made of it. The cast exactly fitted one of her shoes. Scientists also found three **gallstones** on the ground near the metal drum. Because they were covered in fat they had resisted the acid. Other identifying discoveries that survived the acid included dentures, the handle of Mrs Durand-Deacon's plastic bag, a lipstick container, a hairpin and a notebook.

IDENTIFYING DENTURES

The forensic team was able to identify the false teeth of Olive Durand-Deacon because the acrylic resin that the teeth were made of would have taken at least three weeks to dissolve. Olive Durand-Deacon's dentist was contacted and he managed to identify the dentures as belonging to her, from his records of her past treatments.

John Haigh (on the right at the top of the steps) leaves court during his trial.

TRIAL AND SENTENCE

Haigh's trial began on 1 July 1949. He was found guilty of murdering Mrs Durand-Deacon and sentenced to death. He was hanged on 10 August.

BORN TO RAISE HELL

Richard Speck was born in Kirkwood, Illinois, USA, in 1941. In his teens, Speck became a heavy drinker. He also took drugs. He dropped out of school and was arrested for trespassing, burglary and stabbing. At 19, Speck had his arm tattooed with the words 'Born to Raise Hell'.

Richard Speck.

NIGHT OF TERROR

On 13 July 1966, at 11 pm, Speck knocked on the door of a house in Chicago. Nine nurses shared the house. The six who were at home thought it was a housemate who had forgotten her key. One of them opened the door to find Speck brandishing a knife. He forced his way in. Speck was heavily under the influence of alcohol and drugs. He held the nurses in the house for several hours. As the other three nurses returned home, Speck took them hostage as well.

One by one Speck either strangled or stabbed eight of the nurses. One of them, a Filipino named Corazon Amurao, managed to escape. She crawled under a bed while Speck was out of the room with one of the other nurses.

SURVIVOR

Amurao stayed under the bed until daylight, unsure if Speck was still in the house. Just before 6 am, Amurao climbed out of the bedroom window and managed to attract the attention of two men in the street. They called the police.

Amurao was taken to the local hospital. Eventually she was well enough to give the police a description of Speck. From her description the police **forensic artist** produced a **composite drawing** of Speck, which was circulated in the area. Amurao also described the tattoo on Speck's arm.

FORENSIC ART

Forensic art is used in many criminal investigations. Artists produce composite images from individually described features to give an impression of a criminal's appearance. Forensic artists are also employed to try to reconstruct faces from unidentified human remains. Sometimes, in cases where suspects or victims have disappeared, forensic artists are asked to artificially age faces from photographs to give investigators a better idea of the missing person's current appearance.

The composite drawing of Speck released by the Chicago Police Department soon after the murders.

17

SCENE OF THE CRIME

The crime scene investigators began to search for clues. The bodies of the nurses were sent for **post-mortem** examinations. Investigators found blood and fingerprints in the house. One of the fingerprints, found on the door of a bedroom, matched one provided by the FBI, which belonged to Richard Speck.

FINGERPRINTING

A fingerprint is the pattern of ridges on the fingertip. Everyone has a unique set of fingerprints, making them an ideal form of identification. There are three main types of fingerprint used for identification. The first is called patent fingerprints and these can clearly be seen. This is usually because the finger has been in blood, ink, oil or some other liquid. The second is called latent fingerprints. These are less visible but can be made clearer by dusting them with powder or applying a chemical. The third type is the impressed print. These are fingerprints that have been made in a soft material that retains the detail of the print. Impressed prints can be photographed.

Crime scene: one of the bedrooms in the nurses' house where Speck committed his murders.

HOSPITAL VISIT

Two days after the murders, Speck was admitted to Cook County Hospital. He had attempted suicide with an overdose of drugs. He was treated by Dr LeRoy Smith, who recognized Speck from the drawing the police had circulated. He also recognized the tattoo on Speck's arm. Dr Smith contacted the police.

Speck was arrested and charged with eight counts of murder. He remained in hospital under police guard. The police arranged for Corazon Amurao to dress as a nurse and go into Speck's room. She identified Speck as the intruder and murderer.

TRIAL AND SENTENCE

Before Speck's trial could begin, he was examined by eight independent psychiatrists. The psychiatrists reported that Speck was fit to stand trial. Speck's trial opened on 20 February 1967. He was found guilty and sentenced to death. In 1972 his sentence was changed to life imprisonment. Speck died in prison in December 1991.

Corazon Amurao (left), the sole survivor of Speck's attack, is reunited with her family.

TED BUNDY

Theodore 'Ted' Bundy was born near Philadelphia, USA, in 1946. He is arguably America's most infamous serial killer. Bundy embarked on his killing spree in 1974 while studying law at the University of Washington in Seattle. Between January and July 1974 nine young girls – most of them students – disappeared in Seattle.

Mass murderer Ted Bundy.

MAN WITH A SLING

In July witnesses gave police a description of a man with a sling who had approached a young girl in a park. A **forensic artist** drew an impression of the man from these descriptions. It was published in the Seattle newspapers. Several people who knew Ted Bundy reported him as a possible suspect. However, these were just a few out of thousands of responses and the police did not follow up the lead.

On 6 September 1974 some human remains were discovered near Seattle. Dental records helped to identify the remains as belonging to Janice Ott and Denise Laslund, two of the missing girls.

UTAH AND COLORADO

By this time, Bundy had moved to Salt Lake City, Utah, where he began attending the University of Utah law school. The disappearances soon began again. Four girls went missing between October and December 1974.

In 1975, Bundy shifted his murderous activities to Colorado. Between January and July, nine girls, aged between 13 and 24, disappeared. Some of the girls vanished without trace. The bodies of others were discovered. They showed signs of having been severely beaten and strangled.

In Colorado, Bundy was arrested and convicted of kidnapping and assaulting Carol DaRonch. She was one of the few to survive an encounter with Bundy, and was able to identify him. The police also hoped to charge him with the murder of another girl, Caryn Campbell, whose hair was found to be very similar to a hair found in Bundy's car.

Highly magnified shafts of human hair. Hair experts are skilled at recognizing the individual characteristics of different people's hair.

HAIR IDENTIFICATION

Human hair has a number of distinctive features, including length, colour, thickness and root appearance. Forensic scientists use a comparison microscope to try to match hair from a crime scene with hair from a suspect or victim. Although human hair shares many of the same qualities, a skilled hair examiner can see microscopic differences between hairs belonging to different people.

TO FLORIDA

While Bundy was awaiting trial for murder, he managed to escape from prison and fled to Florida. Here he soon recommenced his killing spree, murdering three more girls and badly maiming three more.

A woman named Nita Neary witnessed a man leaving the homes of Lisa Levy and Martha Bowman, two of Bundy's victims, on 15 January 1978. Neary called the police, who found the bodies of the two girls in their beds. The police could find no fingerprints in the room. But they did find a bite mark on Lisa Levy. This proved to be a crucial piece of evidence.

ARREST AND TRIAL

Ted Bundy was arrested on 15 February 1978. He went on trial in June 1979. Nita Neary's positive identification of Bundy and the bite mark on Lisa Levy together helped to establish his guilt.

A **forensic odontologist** called Dr Richard Souviron gave evidence in court. He showed the jury a blown-up photo of the bite mark. He laid over it a transparent sheet with an enlarged photo of Bundy's teeth. Some of his teeth were chipped or unevenly aligned. It was obvious to the jury that Bundy's distinctive teeth matched the bite mark.

Carol DaRonch, who survived an attack by Bundy, gives evidence at his trial.

Ted Bundy was found guilty and sentenced to death. Bundy was executed in Florida in January 1989. Before he died, he confessed to 30 murders.

FORENSIC DENTISTRY

The Ted Bundy case was the first time that evidence obtained through forensic dentistry had been used in a Florida law court. Forensic odontologists compare the dental impressions taken from someone's mouth with bite mark impressions on the skin. They look for similar indents, pits and cuts. Often this is done through computer-enhanced photography. They can also analyse bite marks on food, for example in cases where a burglar has taken a bite out of some food in a victim's house.

Bundy claimed that he only chipped his tooth in March 1978, after killing Lisa Levy, so the odontologist's evidence was wrong. But this photo, taken in August 1977, clearly shows Bundy with a chipped tooth.

THE WOOD CHIPPER

Richard Crafts was born in New York City in 1937. He grew up to become an airline pilot. In 1975 he married a Danish-born air stewardess called Helle. They bought a house in Newtown, Connecticut, and went on to have three children. But things were not good. Richard was having affairs with other women. In 1986, Helle decided she wanted a divorce and employed a private detective called Keith Mayo to find evidence that Richard was having an affair.

Richard Crafts.

VANISHED

On 20 November 1986 Helle went missing. However, Crafts did not report her disappearance to the police. Keith Mayo was convinced that Helle would not just disappear. He contacted the local police.

When questioned by the police, Crafts claimed that he and Helle had argued and she had walked out. However, Crafts was saying different things to different people. He told the au pair Dawn Thomas that Helle had gone to Denmark to be with her sick mother.

SEARCHING THE HOUSE

Their suspicions aroused, the police obtained a warrant to search Crafts' home. They were astounded by what they found. Crafts possessed a large number of pistols, handguns, hand grenades and ammunition. The police took away the weapons, as well as towels, samples of fibres and a mattress, for closer examination. Forensic scientist Dr Henry Lee carried out a **luminal test** in various parts of the house. It tested positive for the presence of blood.

Back at his laboratory, Dr Lee tested the towels and bedding. On them he found samples of type O-positive blood, the same **blood group** as Helle. But the police could do nothing without Helle's body.

Private investigator Keith Mayo was the first to raise the alarm about Helle Crafts' disappearance.

LUMINAL TEST

To carry out a luminal test, a serologist (blood specialist) will spray an area with special chemicals. In the darkness the sprayed area will turn bright blue if blood is present. The luminal test is highly sensitive and can even detect blood that has been diluted in water.

25

A WITNESS

A breakthrough occurred on 30 December. A snowplough driver called Joseph Hine told police he had seen someone using a wood-chipping machine near the river close to Crafts' house on the night of 20 November. Detectives had already learned from Crafts' credit card statements that he had rented a wood chipper in a nearby town the previous day.

GRUESOME FINDS

The police thoroughly searched the area where the wood chipper had been seen. They found 56 tiny fragments of bone, cloth,

Crafts hired a wood chipper similar to this one.

hair, a piece of a toe, a fragment of fingernail and a letter. In the river they found strands of blonde hair and a chainsaw.

The police arrested Crafts in January 1987. The forensic team's research indicated that Crafts had killed his wife in the bedroom and had then frozen her body in the basement freezer. After cutting her body up with the chainsaw he had taken the pieces to the wood chipper and shredded her. Because the wood chipper was close to the river, the bulk of her remains had blown into the water.

FORENSIC EVIDENCE

Dr Lee testified at Crafts' trial. Forensic tests had proved that the pieces of bone, hair, tissue and nail had been shredded using the same wood-chipping machine.

In the teeth of the chainsaw, scientists found strands of Helle's hair and fibres that matched a rug from Crafts' home. The chainsaw's serial number matched the one that Richard Crafts had bought in 1981.

FIBRE ANALYSIS

Forensic scientists use various tests to try to match fibres. First, colour and physical appearance are compared using a comparison microscope. The test is then repeated under different kinds of light. Sometimes colours can appear the same in ordinary light, but differences show up under infrared and ultraviolet light. Infrared spectrometry is the most precise test. It measures the amount of infrared light that is absorbed when it passes through a fibre. If the results are the same for two fibres, scientists have found a definite match.

Magnified photos of clothing fibres found at a crime scene. The fibres can be compared to fibre samples taken from the suspect to try to find a match.

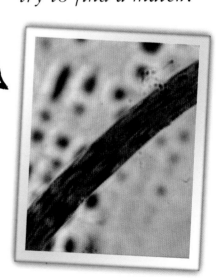

TRIAL AND SENTENCE

In 1990 Richard Crafts was found guilty of murder and sentenced to 99 years imprisonment.

THE NIGHT STALKER

Richard Ramirez was born in El Paso, Texas, in 1960. In his teens he became a heavy drug user and petty thief. In 1978 he moved to California. Six years later, Ramirez began to kill people.

Richard Ramirez, known as the Night Stalker.

FIRST VICTIM

His first murder took place on 28 June 1984. The victim was Jennie Vincow, aged 79. Ramirez stabbed her to death in her apartment in Glassell Park, Los Angeles. Police found fingerprints on the windowsill, but no other leads.

ON THE RAMPAGE

On 17 March 1985 Ramirez struck again. He accosted Angela Barrios in the garage of her apartment building in Rosemead, Los Angeles. Angela was lucky to survive. Ramirez shot her, but the keys she was holding deflected the bullet. Her flatmate, Dayle Okazaki, was not so fortunate. Ramirez shot her in the head. The police found Ramirez's baseball cap in the garage of their house.

That same night, Ramirez killed Tsia-Lian Yu. He pulled her out of her car in Monterey Park and shot her. The police retrieved a metal medallion and a torn

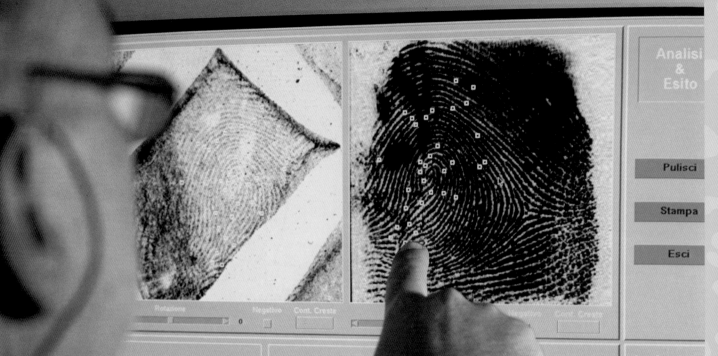

A forensic scientist uses a computer to analyse the characteristic features of a fingerprint, indicated by the yellow spots.

section of a $20 note from the crime scene. Three days later, Ramirez murdered an eight-year-old girl in Eagle Rock.

A week later, Ramirez killed Peter and Maxine Zazzara in their home in Whittier, California. The police found footprints of a tennis shoe in the flowerbeds outside their home.

FINGERPRINT EVIDENCE

Sweat, body oils and dirt mix to leave latent fingerprints on smooth surfaces. Fingerprint identification and matching has been greatly helped by computers. Fingerprints can be analysed and compared with millions of other fingerprints in a computer database in a matter of minutes. Computers can also be programmed to work out a complete fingerprint from fragments.

In May Ramirez attacked Harold and Jean Wu. Harold died in hospital from a gunshot wound, but Jean survived and was able to give the police a physical description of Ramirez.

THE KILLINGS CONTINUE

Ramirez continued attacking and killing through the summer. He became known in Los Angeles as the Night Stalker.

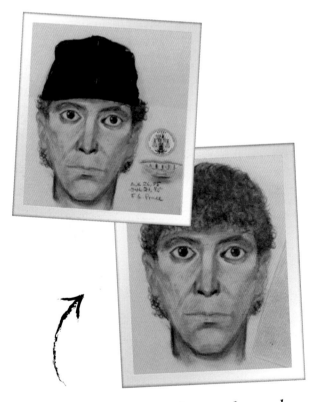

Los Angeles police released a composite drawing of Ramirez, based on Jean Wu's description of him.

In August Ramirez moved to San Francisco. On the 18th he shot Peter and Barbara Pan in the head. He had written 'Jack the Knife' on their wall in lipstick. The forensic team removed a bullet from Peter's head and sent it to the forensic team in Los Angeles. The bullet matched those they had removed from Ramirez' victims there.

One of his victims, who had survived his attack, saw Ramirez leaving the crime scene in an orange Toyota car. She took the license plate number and reported it to the police. When the police found the car, a forensic team searched it for evidence and found a fingerprint. Their computerized fingerprint records matched the fingerprint to Ramirez. The print also matched the one on Jennie Vincow's windowsill from 1984.

CAPTURED

Finally, on 31 August 1985, the police managed to track Ramirez down in Los Angeles. They had been alerted by residents who recognized his face from a photo

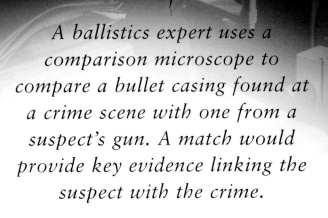

A ballistics expert uses a comparison microscope to compare a bullet casing found at a crime scene with one from a suspect's gun. A match would provide key evidence linking the suspect with the crime.

published in the newspapers. It was nearly three years before Ramirez' trial took place. In addition to the fingerprint and tennis shoe print evidence, **ballistics** evidence was also given in court.

SENTENCE

Richard Ramirez was found guilty of 13 murders, five attempted murders, 11 sexual assaults and 14 burglaries. He was sentenced to death.

BALLISTICS

Every gun leaves its own unique traces at a crime scene. It is the job of the ballistics team to analyse this evidence in order to work out what happened and identify the gun used. The interior of a gun's barrel has grooves that leave striation marks on discharged bullets. These marks can help the ballistics team identify the gun the bullet has been fired from.

HOLLYWOOD MURDER MYSTERY

Los Angeles police were called to the Hollywood home of Roland Kuster, a 37-year-old photographer, on 9 May 1997. A window of the house had been broken. The police also noticed a drop of blood and a bloody footprint from what looked like a trainer. Upstairs, Kuster was dead on his bed. The whole room was splattered with blood and broken glass.

Roland Kuster did photography for brochures and catalogues, but had dreams of working with top models and actors.

COLLECTING THE EVIDENCE

Neighbours reported seeing a man jump over Kuster's fence. The man had been carrying a pair of shoes. The police found a smear of blood on the fence and the front door. The **pathologist** carried out a **post-mortem** on Kuster. Interestingly, he was clutching some hair in his hand.

The police took blood samples. They also photographed the bloody shoeprint. A backpack that they found in Kuster's bedroom contained a letter from a David Minor, sent while Minor had been in prison.

THE POST-MORTEM

Post-mortems of victims of violent crimes are carried out to discover the cause and circumstances of death. Kuster had received 13 stab wounds, mostly to the neck, and suffered blunt force to the head and neck. Based on the wounds, the medical examiner was able to conclude the following: the killer had accosted Kuster in his bedroom, hitting him on the back and over the head with a figurine and repeatedly punching him in the face. This was followed by a wild knife attack that Kuster had tried to fend off. All the wounds occurred while he was still alive.

DEAD ENDS

The police interviewed four people who had been at Kuster's house the night before. They took fingerprints, blood and **DNA** samples from each of them. The investigation of the four friends failed to lead anywhere, however. The police searched their homes, but none of their shoes matched the bloody footprint. The friends' fingerprints were found at Kuster's house, but not near any blood. Their DNA did not match any found at the house. And the hair in Roland's hand turned out to be his own.

Crime scene evidence, such as the bloody shoeprint found at Kuster's house, is carefully recorded by forensic scientists. They photograph the evidence alongside a ruler to provide an accurate scale.

A SUSPECT

The police then contacted the prison service about David Minor. They asked for his fingerprints, but when they arrived they did not match any found in Kuster's house.

David Minor had a long history of armed robbery, assault and burglary. He had been released from prison four days before Roland's murder.

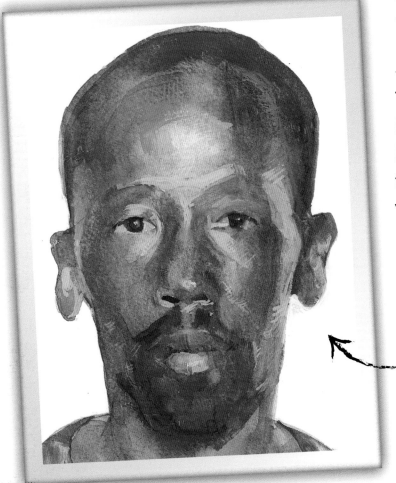

MATCHING THE DNA

The police put out a warrant for Minor's arrest. He was found at the end of July when he tried to enter a homeless shelter. DNA samples were taken from him. A possible match was found between Minor's DNA and that found on some blood samples taken from Kuster's house.

To achieve a more definite match, the forensic team used a specialized test called restriction fragment length polymorphism (RFLP). When the results arrived, they showed a perfect match. The chance of the blood samples belonging to anyone other than David Minor was one in two trillion. Minor was charged with murder.

David Minor had actually been stopped by local police just a few blocks from Kuster's house on the night of the murder. He had been trespassing in someone's garden. They let him go with a warning.

RESTRICTION FRAGMENT LENGTH POLYMORPHISM

Restriction fragment length polymorphism (RFLP) is a technique used to analyse a DNA sample. Special proteins called restriction enzymes break up the sample into fragments. Each fragment is a DNA sequence, a particular ordering of the chemicals within DNA. Analysing these sequences helps to identify a DNA sample or match it to another one.

TRIAL AND SENTENCE

At his trial, the **prosecution** outlined the most likely scenario. David Minor had broken into Roland Kuster's house intending to steal something. But Kuster had disturbed him and a fight had broken out. Minor had killed Kuster and fled the scene, but he forgot to take his backpack. This, together with Minor's blood found at the scene, was enough to convict him. He was found guilty and sentenced to life imprisonment.

This DNA sequence has been produced using RFLP.

BUG EVIDENCE

On 9 July 1997 Kevin Neal reported to the police that his two children had gone missing. He told them that India (11) and Cody (4) had been playing in the garden of his house in Champaign County, Ohio, USA.

GROWING SUSPICIONS

The police began searching the area but could find no sign of the children. There had been family problems and the police were suspicious that Kevin Neal or his wife were responsible for the children's disappearance. The police interviewed the neighbours. They had not heard the children playing outside that day.

Neal told the police that the car in his drive did not work. He said he had not driven it for more than a month. But neighbours confirmed that it had not been in the drive on the day the children disappeared.

Another reason to suspect Neal was his criminal past. He had twice been convicted of assaults on women.

A GRISLY DISCOVERY

On 6 September Andrew Stickley was working on his farm in Nettle Creek, Ohio. As his tractor passed near a cemetery bordering the farm, Andrew caught a smell of decay. He went into the cemetery to investigate and discovered the bodies of two children. Andrew called the police. The bodies were soon identified as those of India and Cody.

The seeds found on Neal's jeans came from Kentucky bluegrass, which grew at the Nettle Creek cemetery, but not at Neal's residence.

36

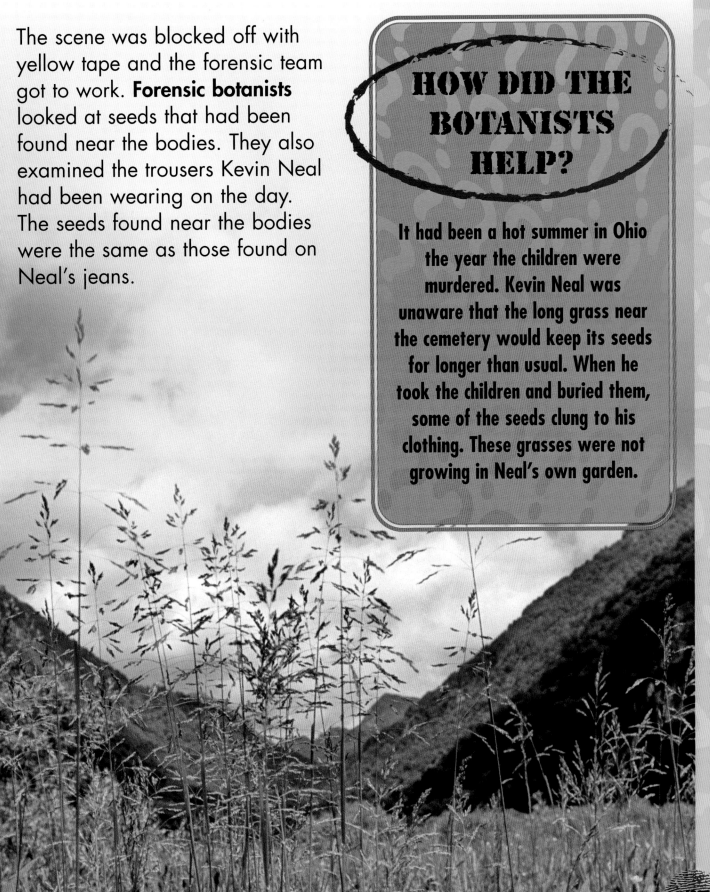

The scene was blocked off with yellow tape and the forensic team got to work. **Forensic botanists** looked at seeds that had been found near the bodies. They also examined the trousers Kevin Neal had been wearing on the day. The seeds found near the bodies were the same as those found on Neal's jeans.

HOW DID THE BOTANISTS HELP?

It had been a hot summer in Ohio the year the children were murdered. Kevin Neal was unaware that the long grass near the cemetery would keep its seeds for longer than usual. When he took the children and buried them, some of the seeds clung to his clothing. These grasses were not growing in Neal's own garden.

37

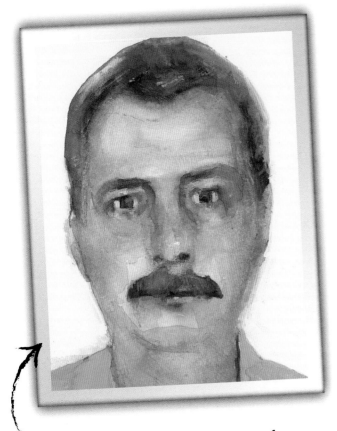

Kevin Neal was a suspect from the start of the investigation.

STUDYING THE INSECTS

Forensic entomologists analysed the insects found inside and around the bodies. By measuring the stages these insects had reached in their life cycles, the entomologists could calculate how long they had been living on the bodies and thereby establish the approximate time of death.

Establishing the time of death was critical in this case because if the children had died after the end of July, Neal could not have been the killer, as he would have been in prison: three weeks after the children disappeared, Neal had been sent to prison for assaulting a woman.

The police warned the media that the forensic analysis could take months. But they were not in any hurry because Kevin Neal, their chief suspect, was behind bars. The case finally went to trial in May 2000.

TIME OF DEATH

Forensic entomologist Dr Neal Haskell gave evidence at the trial. He was one of the first people to apply entomology to criminal investigations. Haskell explained to the jury how the life cycle of a fly can help to establish the time of death. Based on his analysis of the insects at the crime scene, he said that the children had died between 9 and 14 July 1997.

SENTENCE

The jury found Neal guilty. He was sentenced to life imprisonment.

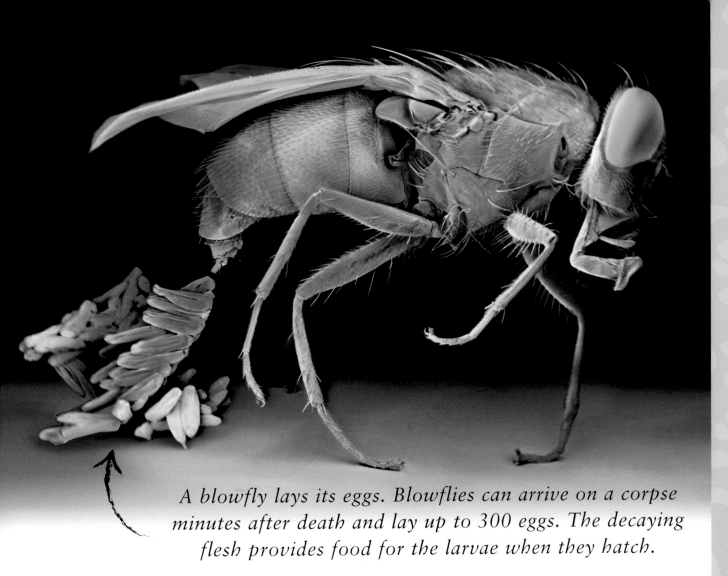

A blowfly lays its eggs. Blowflies can arrive on a corpse minutes after death and lay up to 300 eggs. The decaying flesh provides food for the larvae when they hatch.

WHAT IS FORENSIC ENTOMOLOGY?

Forensic entomologists use their knowledge of insects' life cycles and behaviour to establish time of death. Certain insects, such as blowflies, cheese skippers and screwworms, are attracted to decomposing bodies. Each type of insect prefers bodies at different stages of decomposition. The speed of their life cycles varies according to the average external temperature. The forensic entomologist takes all these factors into account when calculating time of death.

MURDER AT THE PIG FARM

During the 1980s and 1990s a large number of women went missing in British Columbia, Canada. In total, around 60 women vanished between 1983 and 2001. In 1998 the Vancouver Police Department set up a special team to investigate the disappearances.

One member of the team, Inspector Kim Rossmo, used a technique called **geographic profiling** to map the disappearances and search for any patterns. In 1999 Rossmo reported an unusual concentration of disappearances in downtown Eastside. This suggested that a **serial killer** might be at work.

THE PIG FARMER

One of several police suspects was a man called Robert Pickton,

Robert Pickton, a local pig farmer, held wild parties in a converted building at his farm to which a number of the missing women had been invited.

who owned a pig farm in Port Coquitlam, British Columbia. Pickton had been charged with the attempted murder of a woman in 1997.

On 5 February 2002 the local police decided to search Pickton's farm after witnesses reported that

An aerial view of Pickton's pig farm.

GEOGRAPHIC PROFILING

Geographic profiling is a technique developed by the Vancouver Police Department in 1995 and now used by police in many parts of the world. Investigators use computers to analyse the locations of a series of connected crimes in order to find any distinctive patterns. This can help them predict where the next crime might occur or work out the most likely areas where the criminal might be found.

he kept illegal firearms there. During the search, police found an asthma inhaler belonging to Sereena Abotsway, one of the missing women. The Vancouver Police Department's team was contacted. Robert Pickton was arrested and charged with murder.

THE FORENSIC TEAM MOVE IN

The forensic team began the huge task of searching Pickton's 5.7-hectare farm for evidence.

Very soon they began to unearth human remains. As these were discovered and identified as the missing women, Pickton was charged with more and more murders. By October 2002 he had been accused of 15 murders.

Excavations continued until October 2004. Investigators found some 3,000 pieces of evidence at the farm. Other forensic experts focused on reconstructing the crime scene by looking at how the bones were scattered around the farm.

THE TRIAL BEGINS

By the time Pickton's trial began in January 2006, he had been charged with 27 murders. However, the judge reduced the number of charges to six. He decided that trying all 27 would be unfair on the jury, as it could take up to two years.

The **prosecution** alleged that Pickton took the women to his home in Port Coquitlam, murdered them, butchered their remains and then disposed of them. The jury were then presented with a great deal of forensic evidence. Human bones, blood, teeth and hair had all been found on the pig farm. **Forensic anthropologists** were able to match the **DNA** found in these samples to the DNA of many of the missing women.

INSECT EVIDENCE

A **forensic entomologist**, Dr Gail Anderson, also gave evidence. By analysing the insects found in the remains of two of the women, she was able to show that they had been left out in the open for several weeks or months before being placed in a freezer where they were found. Insects had entered the remains before they were put into the freezer. The type of insect and their stage of development helped scientists date the deaths.

In their search for evidence, investigators used conveyor belts to sift through tonnes of earth at Pickton's farm.

TEETH AND DNA

Some of the murder victims on Pickton's farm were identified by their teeth. Teeth are a good source of DNA. The enamel protects the inside of the tooth. When the inside is mixed with liquid nitrogen, it can be crushed to produce a fine powder. This powder can then be tested for DNA.

SENTENCE

Pickton's trial finally ended in December 2007. The jury found Pickton guilty and the judge sentenced him to life imprisonment with no likelihood of release for 25 years.

A scientist removes tissue from a tooth in order to extract a sample of the DNA.

TIMELINE

1835 Henry Goddard of Britain's Scotland Yard is the first to prove a bullet was fired from a particular gun.

1884 The first use of forensic evidence in a violent crimes case: John Toms shot a man with a pistol and the wound in the victim's head contained newspaper. This newspaper was matched with some found in Tom's pockets.

1889 French professor Alexandre Lacassagne links a bullet from a murder scene with a revolver by counting the number of grooves in the revolver's barrel and matching this to marks on the bullet.

1891 Austrian Hans Gross suggests that traces of hair, dust, footprints and fibres can help track down a criminal.

1892 Sir Francis Galton publishes *Finger Prints*, which describes different patterns of fingerprints and shows that no two people have the same fingerprints.

1892 Fingerprint evidence is used in a trial in Argentina to convict a woman of murdering her children.

1897 Edward Richard Henry solves a murder in India by proving that a bloody thumbprint belongs to the murderer.

1901 German scientist Paul Uhlenhuth discovers a means of distinguishing human blood from animal blood.

1901 Karl Landsteiner of Austria discovers the different blood groups.

1904 In the first case solved by trace evidence, German scientist Georg Popp proves that Karl Laubach committed murder on the evidence of a handkerchief left at the scene.

1910 Edmond Locard sets up the first police crime laboratory in France.

1910 Rosella Rousseau is convicted of murdering Germaine Bichon because of hair found at the scene. Victor Balthazard, the French medical examiner, proves that the hair Germaine was clutching came from Rosella's head.

1913 Victor Balthazard makes advances in bullet identification. He is the first to use enlarged photographs to identify bullets.

1915 Italian Leone Lattes finds a way of testing the blood group of dried blood.

1936 John Fiorenza is found guilty of murdering the New York writer Nancy Evans Titterton on the basis of hair and fibre evidence.

1977 The world's first computerized fingerprint database is established in the United States.

1983-4 DNA testing is developed in the United States and Britain.

1987 Colin Pitchfork of Britain, who murdered two girls, is the first criminal to be convicted through DNA evidence.

1990s The National Integrated Ballistic Identification Network (NIBIN), a national database for identifying bullets and guns, is developed in the United States.

1991 Canada develops the first Integrated Ballistics Imaging System (IBIS). It compares the different marks on bullets and shells.

1998 American scientists create the Combined DNA Index System, which allows crime laboratories across the United States to compare DNA samples with a national database.

GLOSSARY

anatomist
An expert in the physical structure of the human body.

ballistics
The study of firearms and ammunition.

blood group
Any of several groups into which human blood is divided.

comparison microscope
A microscope that shows two things at the same time so that they can be compared.

composite drawing
A drawing made up of several elements.

DNA
A chemical molecule that carries genetic information; everyone's DNA is slightly different and so it can be used to identify a particular individual.

forensic anthropology
The application of the study of the human skeleton to criminal investigations. Forensic anthropologists help to identify human remains by using their expertise to establish things like sex, age and health.

forensic artists
Artists who use their skills to help in a criminal investigation. They can produce composite drawings from witness descriptions, age progressions from photos and facial reconstructions from skeletal remains.

forensic botanists
Scientists who apply the study of plant life to criminal investigations. Forensic botanists examine leaves, seeds and pollen found at crime scenes to work out timeframes and whether a body has been moved between different locations. They can also match plant fragments to those found on a suspect.

forensic entomology
The application of the study of insect life to criminal investigations. Forensic entomologists examine insects found in and around dead bodies in order to establish time and place of death.

forensic odontologist
Forensic odontologists, or dentists, can help to identify human remains by matching teeth to existing dental records. They are also able to match bite marks, for example in food discarded at a crime scene, to the teeth of suspects.

gallstone
A small hard mass that forms inside the gallbladder, often as a result of infection. The gallbladder is a small muscular sac that forms part of the human digestive system.

geographic profiling
A technique that uses computers to map locations of similar crimes in order to work out where the criminal is located or might strike next.

infrared
Radiation (energy waves) with wavelengths longer than visible light but shorter than radio waves.

infrared spectrometry
A method used to measure how much infrared light is absorbed when passing through a transparent substance. This measurement, known as a 'signature' can be compared to the 'signatures' of other known substances as a way of identifying the unknown substance.

luminal test
A test used to detect the presence of blood on a piece of material.

pathologist
Pathologists perform post-mortems to work out how and why a person died.

post-mortem
An examination of a dead body in order to establish cause and circumstances of death.

prosecution
Lawyers in a court of law who try to prove that the defendant carried out a crime.

serial killer
Someone who murders a number of people over a period of time, especially someone who uses the same method each time.

serologist
An expert in blood serum, the liquid part of blood.

striations
Marks on bullets caused by the parallel grooves inside gun barrels.

sulphuric acid
A powerful, colourless, oily acid used in the manufacture of products such as fertilizers, explosives, detergents and dyes.

superimpose
Place something on top of something else.

trace evidence
Small pieces of evidence found at a crime scene, such as hair, fibre, grass, glass, soil, blood spots and skin.

ultraviolet
Radiation (energy waves) with wavelengths shorter than visible light but longer than x-rays.

x-ray
Radiation (energy waves) with wavelengths shorter than ultraviolet light. X-rays are mainly used in medicine to see inside the body.

FURTHER INFORMATION

BOOKS
CSI Expert!: Forensic Science for Kids by Karen K Shulz (Prufrock Press, 2008)
Forensic Science by Chris Cooper (DK Publishing, 2008)
Gut-Eating Bugs: Maggots Reveal the Time of Death! by Danielle M Denega (Franklin Watts, 2007)
Graphic Forensic Science: Crime Scene Investigators by Rob Shone (Rosen Central, 2008)
Hair, Clothing, and Tire Track Evidence: Crime-Solving Science Experiments by Kenneth G Rainis (Enslow Publishers, 2006)
Science Quest: The Search for Forensic Evidence by Brian Innes (Gareth Stevens Publishing, 2005)

WEBSITES
www.explainthatstuff.com/forensicscience.html
Explains forensic science and suggests activities to do at home.

www.fbi.gov/fbikids.htm
Website set up by the FBI for children, which shows what the force does.

www.cyberbee.com/whodunnit/crime.html
Find out if you can follow the forensic clues and solve the crimes on this website.

www.all-about-forensic-science.com/science-for-kids.html
This website is full of general information about forensic science.

INDEX

Page numbers in **bold** refer to illustrations.